# what's next?

*Important Steps for New Believers*

DISCIPLESHIP SERIES

Published by

HELP4U PUBLICATIONS

CHESTERTON, IN

## HELP4U
PUBLICATIONS

Help4U Publications, LLC
Chesterton, IN 46304

*What's Next?* by David J. Olson
Copyright © 2013 by David J. Olson

ISBN 978-1-940089-05-08

Cover Photo: Lightstock

www.help4Upublications.com

All rights reserved. No part of this publication may be reproduced or transmitted in any form, except for brief quotation in review, without written permission from the publisher.

All Scripture quotations are from the *King James Bible*.

# WHAT'S FIRST?

Before we can discover what's next, we must first consider what comes first. Have you received the Lord Jesus Christ as your Savior? If so, this book is for you! However, just in case someone reading this is not certain about going to heaven, let's quickly review how a person is saved.

*First, understand that you have sinned against God.* We are told, *"For all have sinned, and come short of the glory of God."* (Romans 3:23) King David had the right idea when he said, *"Against thee, thee only, have I sinned, and done this evil in thy sight..."* (Psalm 51:4) Have you realized that many of your attitudes and actions have offended God?

*Second, realize that God punishes sin.* Although God loves you, He hates your sin. Because He is holy, He cannot allow you into heaven unless your sin is cleansed. The Scripture says, *"For the wages of sin is death; but the gift of God is eternal life through Jesus Christ our Lord."* (Romans 6:23) What you and I have earned because of our sinful ways is eternal death. This is described in Revelation 20:14, *"And death and hell were cast into the lake of fire. This is the second death."* God wants to save you from this punishment, but you first have to admit that you are guilty and deserving of hell. Have you ever realized that you were on your way to hell because of your sin? You cannot be saved until you do so.

*Third, stop trusting the wrong thing for salvation.* Many people agree that they are sinners, but they somehow think that God will not judge them because they have done some good thing in life. What do you think will prevent you from going to hell? The truth is that no good works that you have done can earn forgiveness. Consider the words of the apostle Paul, *"For by grace are ye saved through faith; and that not of yourselves: it is the gift of God: Not of works..."* (Ephesians 2:8-9) Because you are a sinner, you have no power to take sin away. You need Jesus for that. If you trust baptism, church attendance, good works, or following the Ten Commandments to be saved, you must change your mind.

*Fourth, turn to Jesus and trust Him for your salvation.* Although you cannot save yourself, Jesus can save you. He did what you cannot do: He paid for your sin. *"For he hath made him to be sin for us, who knew no sin; that we might be made the righteousness of God in him."* (II Corinthians 5:21) On the cross, your sin was placed on Jesus, and He was punished for your sin. If you receive Him, He will remove your sin and give you His righteousness. Once He makes you righteous, you are fit for heaven! So, whose righteousness do you have: His or your own?

If you honestly do not believe you have received Jesus as your Savior, I urge you to do so right now. If you are willing to repent of your sin and self-righteousness, the Lord is willing to save you. Simply call out to Him, confessing that you are a sinner and cannot save yourself. Then, ask Jesus to save you! If you believe that He will save you, He will do it. *"For whosoever shall call upon the name of the Lord shall be saved."* (Romans 10:13)

After getting the matter of salvation settled, you may be wondering, "What's next?" The rest of this book will begin to answer that very question. Are you ready to learn some valuable lessons that will help your relationship with the Lord? Let's get started!

# Chapter One

# Know What You Got!

*"Therefore if any man be in Christ, he is a new creature: old things are passed away; behold, all things are become new."* II Corinthians 5:17

Have you ever bought a new electronic device and began using it without reading the owner's manual? You might figure out a few of the basic features, but you will never take full advantage of all that it can do because you don't really know what you got. That is okay to do with a camera but not with your salvation! Those who don't take the time to study the manual for the Christian life, the Bible, will live a life of trial and error—mostly error. This leads to a disappointing, unproductive life. See for yourself what God's Word teaches about what you got the day you were saved.

## You Got Eternal Life

God gives eternal life to all who trust Jesus for their salvation. John 10:28 says, *"And I give unto them eternal life; and they shall never perish, neither shall any man pluck them out of my hand."* What does the word *eternal* mean? It means without end, endless.  Therefore, if you were given eternal life, it can never end!  I like the simplicity of the Bible, don't you?

The devil wants you to live in fear of losing your salvation, but true salvation can never be lost.  Notice that Jesus promises, *"...they shall **never** perish."*  Never means never!  It cannot happen.  Unfortunately, some churches teach that you can lose your salvation, but this false teaching robs you of confidence in the promise of God.  It is Jesus Who saves us and keeps us saved.  We do not get saved by our good works, and we do not stay saved by them either.  Those who wonder if they still are saved fail to enjoy all of the benefits that come with salvation.  Therefore, be sure that you know what you got!

## YOU GOT FORGIVENESS OF SINS

Many people struggle with guilt concerning their past.  Have you ever felt guilty about something even after you asked God to forgive you?  Why would you still feel guilty?  Well, either you never got forgiveness or you failed to realize the forgiveness you received.

The word *forgive* means to send away.  Jesus came to take away all your sins: *"And ye know that he was manifested to take away our sins; and in him is no sin."* (I John 3:5)  If you have received Jesus as your Savior, your sins have been taken away!  There is no need to continue to feel guilty and defeated any more.  Satan would like you to feel dejected and worthless, but God has cleaned you up.

What about the really big sins?  Are we forgiven of those, too?  The Scripture is quite clear that *"the blood of Jesus Christ his Son cleanseth us from **all** sin."* (I John 1:7)  If we are forgiven of all sin, we are entirely cleansed of it.

What happens if we sin after getting saved? Thankfully, we do not lose our salvation. However, we do lose our closeness to God. It's like a child who has disobeyed his parents and does not feel that same freedom in their presence as he once enjoyed. After the child apologizes, the nearness is reinstated. God says, *"If we confess our sins, he is faithful and just to forgive us our sins, and to cleanse us from all unrighteousness."* (I John 1:9) Isn't it great that God promises to make us clean if we acknowledge and confess our wrongdoing?

## You Got a New Family

If you received Jesus as your Savior, you were born again into God's family. Now you can enjoy all the family privileges. What are some of the blessings we get?

*First of all, we gain a Heavenly Father.* Contrary to popular belief, we are not born as children of God. Oh, it is true that He is the Creator of all, but He is not the Father of all. Before

> WE HAVE A HEAVENLY FATHER WHO LOVES US AND WANTS THE BEST FOR US.

salvation, the devil was your father, and you were under his rule. Following Satan got us all in a lot of trouble, but now we are set free from his bondage and have been adopted into God's family. Thankfully, we have a new Father Who loves us and wants the best for us, delighting to bless us: *"If ye then, being evil, know how to give good gifts unto your children, how much more shall your Father which is in heaven give good things to them that ask him?"* (Matthew 7:11)

*Second, we receive Heavenly provision.* A good father provides for the needs of his children, and God will do the same for His children. Matthew 6:32-33 says, *"...for your heavenly Father knoweth that ye have need of all these things. But seek ye first the kingdom of God, and his righteousness; and all these things shall be added unto you."* There is no need to worry about food, clothing, housing, or anything! Of course, God expects you to work, but He will supply all your needs if you trust Him. Never let the devil cause you to worry.

*Third, we receive Heavenly correction.* All good parents correct their children. God loves His children so much that He does not allow us to continue in activities that are harmful to us. He lovingly corrects us through chastisement. Hebrews 12:6 says, *"For whom the Lord loveth he chasteneth, and scourgeth every son whom he receiveth."* Although you will never lose your salvation after getting saved, that does not mean you will never be corrected! A heavenly swat is often administered by God to get our attention. His goal is to prevent us from travelling too far down the path of sin, which will lead to eventual heartache and sorrow. Such correction may come through problems with our health, job, finances, or family. Afflictions are meant to help us, not hurt us. David's testimony was, *"Before I was afflicted I went astray: but now have I kept thy word."* (Psalm 119:67)

## YOU GOT A CHANGED LIFE

The Godhead consists of three persons: the Father, the Son, and the Holy Spirit. The moment a person receives Christ, a wonderful change occurs. The Holy Spirit enters, washes, and renews. Titus 3:5 explains, *"Not by works of righteousness which we have done, but according to his mercy he saved us, by the washing of regeneration, and renewing of the Holy Ghost."*

When you received Jesus, He sent His Holy Spirit into your life to live with you. *"Know ye not that ye are the temple of God, and that the Spirit of God dwelleth in you?"* (I Corinthians 3:16) He goes where you go, and you won't feel comfortable around sinful activities like you once did.

Many changes occur in your heart when you get saved. Paul said, *"Therefore if any man be in Christ, he is a new creature: old things are passed away; behold, all things are become new."* (II Corinthians 5:17) All things in your life are new! You get new desires, a new understanding of the Bible, a new conviction of sin, new attitudes, a new sense of joy, a new concern for others, a new purpose in life, and a new future.

When do you think these changes should begin in your life? Obviously, they start the moment you are saved. You won't be perfect, but you will notice a difference within your heart. If there is absolutely no change, you never got salvation. However, if you have seen changes since you received Christ, be encouraged that God will continue to transform you throughout your entire life as you yield to Him. *"Being confident of this very thing, that he which hath begun a good work in you will perform it until the day of Jesus Christ."* (Philippians 1:6)

## SUMMARY

Isn't it great to know a little more of what you got? You got eternal life that cannot end, forgiveness of all sins, a new family, and a changed life with promise of more change!

# Chapter Two

# Begin to Grow

*"As newborn babes, desire the sincere milk of the word, that ye may grow thereby: If so be ye have tasted that the Lord is gracious."* I Peter 2:2-3

When a baby is born, nobody expects him to remain the same size. Growth is expected, and we would be concerned if a child failed to develop. Usually, if we haven't seen a child for a few months, we are surprised to see how much he has changed when we do see him again.

When a person receives Christ as Savior, he becomes a child of God. Although he may be an adult physically, the new believer is a babe spiritually and, as such, needs to grow. Peter said we are as *"newborn babes"* requiring spiritual nourishment.

One of your utmost goals in life should be to grow up into a healthy, productive Christian. Failure to grow will result in a weak, pathetic existence. Babies can do little for themselves and are dependent upon all around them. Certainly, that is not a good condition to be in spiritually. Let's consider some questions about growing for God.

# WHY SHOULD WE GROW?

*Growth is natural.* As we look around God's creation, we see many examples of growth. When a seed is planted, it germinates, shoots up, and produces fruit. A little puppy in a matter of months becomes a big dog. Tiny tadpoles quickly turn into frogs. Fluffy day-old chicks grow so rapidly that they are on a person's plate in just a few weeks. Growth can be fast or slow, but it always occurs where there is life. So, if you have new life in Christ, you will grow; and growing at a healthy rate depends upon you. Some Christians grow faster than others, and much of that hinges on their desire for spiritual nourishment.

*Growth is exciting.* When you ask a twelve-year-old, "How old are you?" he usually says, "I'm **going to be** thirteen." Why? Most kids are looking forward to getting older. As growth brings more opportunities and excitement in the life of a young person, spiritual maturity in the Christian brings more opportunities to serve the Lord. God has a place for you to serve in His church, and you ought to look forward to what He has next for your life! Notice the great disappointment expressed toward those who failed to grow properly: *"For when for the time ye ought to be teachers, ye have need that one teach you again which be the first principles of the oracles of God; and are become such as have need of milk, and not of strong meat."* (Hebrews 5:12) They should have matured to *"meat"* but still needed *"milk"* like infants. Let us not be limited in our service for God because of stunted growth. Wouldn't you rather be treated as an adult than as a baby?

*Growth is commanded.* Since growth is both natural and exciting, it seems odd that we would have to be commanded to do it. Nevertheless, we are reminded to do so, *"But grow in grace, and in the knowledge of our Lord and Saviour Jesus Christ."* (II Peter 3:18) So, what hinders our growth? Unfortunately, we do not always have an appetite for spiritual matters and, at times, would rather fulfill our fleshly cravings. No man can feast on carnality and spirituality at the same time. For instance, someone who enjoys reading filthy novels or magazines does not enjoy reading the Bible. We must learn to hunger for the right things. Jesus told us, *"Blessed are they which do hunger and thirst after righteousness: for they shall be filled."* (Matthew 5:6) Once full, we begin to grow! Therefore, all sinful pleasures spoil our growth and must be denied. God's command to grow reminds us that we have a responsibility to advance in our faith, and failing to do so is sin.

## IN WHAT AREAS SHOULD WE GROW?

The apostle Peter told of two areas in which we should grow. Once again, we refer to II Peter 3:18, *"But grow in grace, and in the knowledge of our Lord and Saviour Jesus Christ."* Grace and knowledge must be our goal. Think of it this way, knowledge tells us what we should do and grace helps us do it.

*Grow in grace.* Grace is favor shown to us by God that is completely undeserved. It enables us to do things we could not normally do. Paul testified, *"But by the grace of God I am what I am: and his grace which was bestowed upon me was not in vain; but I laboured more abundantly than they all: yet not I, but the grace of God which was with me."* (I Corinthians 15:10) Three times in this one verse he states that God's grace empowered him to work for the Lord. We may plan and purpose to serve God, but the only way to receive overcoming strength is through obtaining more grace. The best thing about grace is that the Lord never runs out of it—*"...he giveth more grace."* (James 4:6)

*Grow in knowledge.* Do you know everything you need to know about God and His will for your life? Obviously not! Thus, you cannot take the command to grow in knowledge casually. A student in school will learn little unless he pays attention, studies, and applies himself. If the student fails to attend school or open his books at home, he is destined for failure. Likewise, a Christian must get serious about studying the Bible. It is our duty to get into the Word of God at home and be in church where the Scriptures are being taught. Do you understand everything about marriage, raising children, getting victory over sin, obtaining answers to prayer, resisting temptation, or telling others how to be saved? If not, grow in knowledge.

## How Can We Grow?

Now, we know why and in what areas we should grow, but how do we do it? God's Word makes it simple:

> *Wherefore laying aside all malice, and all guile, and hypocrisies, and envies, and all evil speakings, As newborn babes, desire the sincere milk of the word, that ye may grow thereby: If so be ye have tasted that the Lord is gracious.* I Peter 2:1-3

Let's consider three tips from the above passage on how we can grow for God.

*Stay healthy.* A child who is always weak and sickly will fail to develop properly. Sickness and disease have prevented millions of children around the world from becoming strong, vibrant adults. However, those who are free from such maladies are generally much stronger and live longer. The key is to not only rid the body of disease but also prevent it. Sin is much like sickness, and it must be removed and guarded against just like a disease. Peter's prescription involved *"laying aside all malice, and all guile, and hypocrisies, and envies, and all evil speakings."* In other words, get the sin out! Growth is always hindered by spiritual disease. What sins may be stunting your growth?

*Eat right.* Doctors always stress that a proper diet is essential to a strong, healthy body. Good nutrition promotes optimal growth. Sadly, children who face malnutrition in developing countries will bear the marks of a poor diet throughout life and be more susceptible to sickness and death. Likewise, we must eat right to avoid spiritual malnutrition! Peter further exhorts, *"As newborn babes, desire the sincere milk of the word, that ye may grow thereby."* What must our diet be? The milk of the Word!

Children who only eat candy and ice cream are never strong and healthy. People today try to live their Christian lives in the same way. They want everything sugarcoated from the pulpit. However, a steady diet of sweets never leads to strong development of the soul. Be sure to desire the milk of the Word more than the sugary teachings of men. Get into a church that serves some substance in the sermons and tries to give you what you need.

*Get some more.* What do you do when you have tasted something wonderful? You want some more! Has God performed some wonderful things in your life since you have been saved? If so, go back to Him and get more. The desire to grow hinges on whether *"ye have tasted that the Lord is gracious."* His cupboard is never empty of necessities, and His pot is always full of blessings! Have you had some victories? Get some more. Have you found joy? Get some more. Have you gotten answers to prayer? Get some more!

# Chapter Three

# Take the Next Step

*"The steps of a good man are ordered by the LORD:
and he delighteth in his way."* Psalm 37:23

Parents get excited over the first steps of their child because it shows that the child is developing and making progress. The first steps we take in our Christian life are also anticipated by our Heavenly Father. His desire is that we mature and learn to move forward in our walk with Him. However, a person can't walk unless he takes his first step! The first step after salvation is baptism.

As our society drifts farther away from God and the teachings of the Bible, it is not surprising that many fail to understand what baptism is all about. We know for certain that baptism has been practiced since the time of Jesus, and history proves that many Christians have been persecuted for it. In fact, tens of thousands have died for their practice of Biblical baptism. So, whatever it is, it must be important!

The Bible makes it clear that we should follow Jesus. Peter tells us, *"For even hereunto were ye called...that ye should follow his steps."* (I Peter 2:21) One of His steps was baptism, and much can be learned by studying this great event in His life. Therefore, we will answer some key questions about baptism as we consider the example and instruction provided by the Master.

## What is Baptism?

Simply stated, baptism is a picture of the death, burial, and resurrection of Jesus. Our Lord came to die for our sins and wanted to leave a memorial of His great sacrifice. He often spoke of His death so that His disciples would remember His purpose in coming. *"And he began to teach them, that the Son of man must suffer many things, and be rejected of the elders, and of the chief priests, and scribes, and be killed, and after three days rise again."* (Mark 8:31) Through baptism Jesus has provided a tangible way for His followers to identify with Him. By being submerged in the water, we picture the death and burial of Jesus. As we come out of the water, we picture His triumphant resurrection.

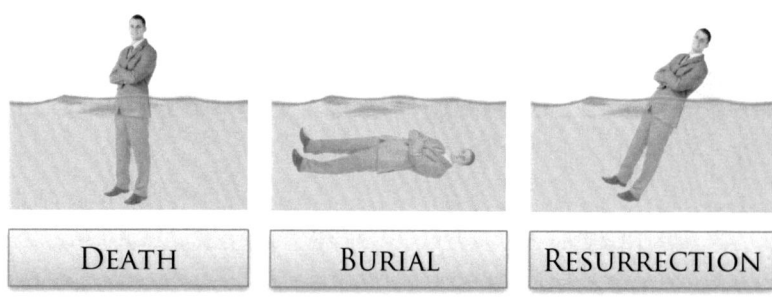

Our baptism shows that we believe that Jesus died, was buried, and rose again for our salvation. Paul describes it in Romans 6:4-5:

> *Therefore we are buried with him by baptism into death: that like as Christ was raised up from the dead by the glory of the Father, even so we also should walk in newness of life. For if we have been*

*planted together in the likeness of his death, we shall be also in the likeness of his resurrection...*

The wording is entirely symbolic. Notice the phrase, *"we are buried with him by baptism."* None of us were literally buried in the tomb with Him. As He was buried in the earth, we are *"buried"* by going under water in baptism. Further, it demonstrates that our salvation brought a death to our old sinful life and created a desire to live a new life for Jesus. Notice further, *"...as Christ was raised...even so we also should walk in newness of life."* His resurrection is a picture of the new life we received when we trusted Him. Our baptism illustrates the change Jesus has made in our lives. In no way do these verses imply that baptism gives us new life. It is Christ Who does that, and baptism is just a picture of it.

Allow me to illustrate this point. A wedding ring is a symbol of marriage much like baptism is of salvation. The wearing of such a ring does not make one married, and getting baptized does not save a person. People can be married without wearing a ring, and people can be saved without being baptized. The ring merely shows that a marriage has taken place, and baptism pictures that we have put our faith in Jesus' work for salvation. A person is not married based on his or her ring, and neither is a person's salvation based upon his baptism. Both simply provide a picture of an important event. Now that we know what baptism is, let's move on to the next question.

## WHY BE BAPTIZED?

Have you ever wondered why Jesus was baptized? Much confusion about baptism could be cleared up by simply taking an honest look at the Scriptures. Before proceeding any further, we must dispel some false teachings about the purpose of baptism. Certain denominations teach that baptism is necessary for salvation. They say that the waters of baptism wash away sin and make a person a child of God. Jesus' baptism refutes both of these ideas. First of all, Jesus had no sin to wash away. Secondly, He was already the Son of God and did not become such by baptism. We can conclude, therefore, that our baptism does not wash away sin or make us a child of God—only faith can save us.

*Baptism is the right thing to do.* John the Baptist was a bit puzzled that Jesus insisted on being baptized; but Jesus answered, *"...thus it becometh us to fulfill all righteousness."* (Matthew 3:15) If it was right for Jesus to provide us with a picture of His death, burial, and resurrection, then it is right for us to identify with Him by observing the memorial. Jesus was not ashamed to own us, and neither should we be ashamed of Him. *"For the scripture saith, Whosoever believeth on him shall not be ashamed."* (Romans 10:11) If getting baptized is right to do, failing to do so is wrong. Do you want to be right or wrong in your relationship with God?

*Baptism pleases God.* Immediately after Jesus was baptized, the Father spoke from Heaven, *"This is my beloved Son, in whom I am well pleased."* (Matthew 3:17) It is obvious that doing the right thing is pleasing to God. When our life pleases Him, He pours out His blessings upon our lives. Failing to be baptized will hinder those blessings.

*Baptism demonstrates obedience.* Jesus taught that the first thing to be done after salvation is baptism. He said, *"Go ye therefore, and teach all nations, baptizing them in the name of the Father, and of the Son, and of the Holy Ghost."* (Matthew 28:19) Peter reinforced this truth with the crowd at Jerusalem when he stated, *"Repent, and be baptized every one of you."* (Acts 2:38) The first command given to a Christian after salvation is to be baptized. Refusing baptism is disobedience. Do you want to be an obedient child or a disobedient one? It will be very difficult for you to take other steps for the Lord if you fail to take the first step!

*Baptism shows love.* A true sign of our love to God is our obedience. Jesus said, *"If ye love me, keep my commandments."* (John 14:15) Since baptism is a command, we cannot properly prove our love to God without getting baptized. Don't you want to show Him how much you love Him? If so, let nothing hinder you from getting baptized.

*Baptism brings joy.* A little child trying to please his dad becomes filled with happiness when he sees the smile on his father's face. Truly, the bond between the Father and Son was glorious the day that Jesus was baptized.

> A DEEP SENSE OF JOY FLOODS THE SOUL WHEN YOU OBEY THE LORD.

Likewise, a deep sense of joy floods our hearts when we obey the Lord. After the Ethiopian man was saved, he got baptized. Notice the result: *"And when they were come up out of the water...he went on his way rejoicing."* (Acts 8:39) Don't you want to go on your way rejoicing?

## How Should We Be Baptized?

*Baptism is by immersion only.* We should get baptized the same way Jesus did—by immersion. He was not sprinkled with water, nor was water poured on Him. He went **into** the Jordan River. The account reads, *"And it came to pass in those days, that Jesus came from Nazareth of Galilee, and was baptized of John in Jordan."* (Mark 1:9) Matthew tells us, *"And Jesus, when he was baptized, went up straightway out of the water."* (Matthew 3:16) Jesus clearly went *"in Jordan"* and came *"out of the water."* There is no hint that anything other than immersion happened. Besides, the meaning of the word *baptize* is *to dip, plunge,* or *immerse.* Since He was baptized, it means that He was plunged under the water. Don't you think your baptism should be performed in the same manner?

## WHEN SHOULD WE BE BAPTIZED?

*Baptism comes after salvation.* In every case in the Bible, baptism came after repentance. In other words, you can only be baptized after receiving Jesus as your Savior. If you were baptized before you were saved, you were not really baptized because you did it for the wrong reason and you need to be baptized Biblically.

God always puts the condition of believing in Christ before baptism. Notice the order of events in Acts 18:8, *"...many of the Corinthians hearing believed, and were baptized."* Which came first: the baptism or believing? Believing! The message is clear—believe first.

*Baptism should not be delayed.* The Ethiopian was baptized as soon as they found some water. The jailor in Philippi was baptized *"the same hour of the night."* (Acts 16:31-33) Three thousand people in Jerusalem got saved and were baptized the same day: *"Then they that gladly received his word were baptized: and the same day there were added unto them about three thousand souls."* (Acts 2:41) The main idea we glean from these accounts is that we should not make excuses to put off baptism. Don't worry if your church requires a baptism class. In such a case, they are not trying to delay your baptism—they merely want to ensure you have a proper understanding. So, make your decision to follow Jesus and be baptized as soon as possible!

# Chapter Four

# Get to Know God

*"That I may know him, and the power of his resurrection"*
Philippians 3:10

Have you ever wondered how to get to know God better? Well, it's really quite simple. Spend time with Him. Just as you become acquainted with someone by conversing together, you can develop a relationship with God the same way. Communication with God is a two-way street. You must learn to talk and listen.

## Talk to God

The way to talk to the Lord is through prayer. You may have been taught to recite memorized prayers or rely on a prayer book to help you, but this is not God's plan for prayer. Jesus warned about this kind of lifelessness in Matthew 6:7, *"But when ye pray, use not vain repetitions, as the heathen do: for they think that they shall be heard for their much speaking."* The word *vain* means empty or useless. God wants heartfelt prayers, not meaningless repetition of the same old thing over and over again.

When we talk to people we love, we open up to them and use warm language. This is how we should communicate with God. Begin to treat Him as a real Person with Whom you can freely talk about anything and everything. Let's consider a couple of ideas that will guide you into a more meaningful prayer life.

*Ask Him for help.* One of the most powerful people in the world is the President of the United States. If you had an urgent matter and tried to see him, you would be stopped by security personnel. However, with God you have direct access! *"Let us therefore come boldly unto the throne of grace, that we may obtain mercy, and find grace to help in time of need."* (Hebrews 4:16) Those words *"help in time of need"* are precious. Asking for help allows you to discover God's character and kindness as He reveals Himself to you through answered prayer. Do you really want to know His sympathy, deliverance, and power? Go ahead and talk to Him!

*Tell Him your problems.* Surely you have troubles in your life of some sort! Don't hold it all inside—learn to talk to God about it. David gives good advice in Psalm 55:22, *"Cast thy burden upon the LORD, and he shall sustain thee."* Why should we be heavily weighed down by our problems when God is ready to lift them off of us? Take the matter to the Lord in prayer. *"Trust in him at all times; ye people, pour out your heart before him: God is a refuge for us."* (Psalm 62:8) Just open up to God and pour out any grief or anguish that is in your heart.

*Ask Him questions.* The way to find out more about a person is to ask him questions. Do you ever read things in the Bible and not understand them? Perhaps certain events or circumstances in your life puzzle you. Ask God about them. He promised, *"Call unto me, and I will answer thee, and shew thee great and mighty things, which thou knowest not."* (Jeremiah 33:3) In His timing, He will let you know what you need to know. Ask Him what He thinks about your friends, activities, attitude, and future plans.

*Thank Him.* To enter into the presence of God, we should come with thankful lips. Psalm 100:4 says, *"Enter into his gates with thanksgiving, and into his courts with praise: be thankful unto him, and bless his name."* Closeness to God requires gratefulness, and God listens to those who appreciate what He has already done for them. To gain an audience with God you must express gratitude.

## LISTEN TO GOD

When conversing with someone wiser than yourself, it is best not to do all the talking. So, be sure you take time to listen to God in addition to praying to Him. Does God really speak to people in the twenty-first century? Oh, yes! He does so through His written Word, the Bible. This Book is like no other because it is God's Word—not man's. It consists of sixty-six books with two major divisions: the Old Testament and the New Testament. The Old Testament records the account of creation and the history of the nation of Israel, including prophecies of a coming Savior. The New Testament reveals Jesus as the promised Savior and provides instructions for those who accept Him. It includes prophecies involving the end of the earth and future judgment. No other book has the power to calm, convince, and comfort because no other book is a direct revelation from God.

No audible voice from Heaven could be more reliable than what is already recorded in the Bible. The apostle Peter heard God's voice one time on the holy mount but concluded that in the Scriptures, *"We have also a more sure word of prophecy."* (II Peter 1:19) The Bible is God's message to all of mankind and should not be neglected. All the answers for life's problems are found in the Bible. Paul said, *"All scripture is given by inspiration of God, and is profitable for doctrine, for reproof, for correction, for instruction in righteousness."* (II Timothy 3:16) Simply put, the message comes from God and helps us with everyday living.

*God speaks through the Scriptures.* As we talk to God through prayer, He talks to us through the Bible. If we fail to learn His Word, we will never get to know Him. Perhaps neglecting your Bible has been the source of many of your problems! Thankfully, God has given us two ways to learn His Word.

> GOD SPEAKS TO US THROUGH THE BIBLE.

First, daily Bible reading allows God to speak to your heart every day. Luke told us of the people in Thessalonica who *"searched the scriptures daily."* (Acts 17:11) How many days in the week do you not need a message from God? None! Determine to make time to read the Bible every morning before you start your day. This will allow God to give you wisdom to face whatever comes your way.

Second, God speaks through the preaching of His Word. Titus 1:2-3 says, *"God, that cannot lie…hath in due times manifested his word through preaching."* Something special happens when a faithful man of God preaches the Word of God in the power of the Spirit of God. It is amazing how the Lord will address the very needs of your heart through preaching. It is not enough to simply stay at home and read the Bible for yourself; you must also go to church to hear His Word preached. God has chosen both methods to speak to us, and ignoring either one will cause us to miss important messages from Him.  Therefore, be faithful to daily Bible reading <u>and</u> be consistent in church attendance.

*God speaks through His Spirit.*  Much confusion has arisen concerning the Holy Spirit of God.  Many people lean on feelings, saying that the Spirit has led them in a certain direction.  However, the Holy Spirit will never lead you contrary to what is written in the Bible.  His job is to *"guide you into all truth."* (John 16:13)  Furthermore, Jesus said, *"...he shall teach you all things, and bring all things to your remembrance, whatsoever I have said unto you."* (John 14:26)  It's simple: the Holy Spirit will speak to your heart and remind you what the Word of God says.  He will impress the truths from Scripture upon your heart and guide you.  However, you must listen to Him.  Don't ignore Him when He prompts you to avoid sin or perform an act of kindness.

## TIPS FOR PRAYER AND BIBLE STUDY

Here are some practical ideas to help you begin communicating with the Lord:

1. Find a quiet place.  (Matthew 6:6, Luke 6:12)
2. Try to be alone.  (Mark 6:46, Matthew 14:23)
3. Choose a time in the morning.  (Psalm 5:3)
4. Spend time with God every day.  (Psalm 86:3)
5. Do not hurry through your time with God.  (Psalm 27:14, Psalm 46:10, Isaiah 40:31)
6. Have a desire to be with God.  (Psalm 119:16)
7. Go to bed early so that you can get up early and spend time with God.  (Psalm 127:2)
8. Have a place to read in your Bible.  (I recommend that new Christians begin reading in the New Testament.  *Proverbs* provides practical wisdom, and *Psalms* lends great comfort.)

## WHAT TO INCLUDE IN YOUR DAILY TIME WITH GOD

Getting to know God does not have to be complicated. The more time you spend with the Lord, the easier it becomes. Here are some pointers about what to include in your daily time with God:

1. Start with a short prayer.
    - ✓ Thank the Lord for His many blessings.
    - ✓ Confess any known sins.
    - ✓ Ask Him to teach you something from the Bible.

2. Read your Bible and think about it.
    - ✓ Look for a message from God to you every day. (Example: a promise, a warning, a blessing, a command, or a fact about God)

3. Write down God's message to you for each day to help you remember. You can use a notebook for this.

4. Have some time for prayer.
    - ✓ Develop a prayer list, including important things such as: personal needs, family needs, friends, church leaders, and people who need to be saved.

5. Keep a journal of blessings and answers to prayer.

If you would like a book designed to help you develop a daily walk with God, I recommend *My Time with God*. It is loaded with many ideas and tools that will help you with your prayer life and Bible reading. *My Time with God* is available from the same publisher as this book.

# Chapter Five

# Beware of Your Enemies

*"Be sober, be vigilant; because your adversary the devil, as a roaring lion, walketh about, seeking whom he may devour"*
I Peter 5:8

Military soldiers are trained to know their enemies. They study their foes' nature, characteristics, and tactics to avoid defeat in the day of battle. You, as a Christian, would be wise to do likewise since you are engaged in spiritual warfare. Whether you realize it or not, you also have enemies that assault your soul; and you must consider who they are and how they attack. Your three main enemies are the devil, your flesh, and this wicked world.

## Beware of Satan

Satan is the most obvious of all our enemies. However, he has been clever enough to hide his true nature from most alive today. Although most people understand the concept of good and evil, Satan has created much confusion about that, too. For instance, people today use the expression, "That is wicked good!" How can something be wicked and good at the same time? Sadly, to many in the world, wickedness is no longer wicked. Abortion is no longer considered to be murder; now it is called pro-choice. Homosexuality is no longer known as an abomination; now it is accepted as an alternative lifestyle. Satan has been so successful in blinding the multitudes about himself that many know little more than his name. We must not remain ignorant of this adversary any longer. Let's consider a few things about him.

The devil is not a myth, nor is he some little man running around in a red suit with a pitchfork. He is very much real. Originally, his name was Lucifer (Isaiah 14:12), and he held an extremely high position in heaven. Speaking to him God said, *"Thou art the anointed cherub that covereth; and I have set thee so: thou wast upon the holy mountain of God...Thou wast perfect in thy ways from the day that thou wast created, till iniquity was found in thee."* (Ezekiel 28:14-15) Lucifer was a perfect angel, but with his free will he chose to sin. In fact, he had aspirations to take over heaven. He was so beautiful and powerful that he actually thought he had a chance to dethrone God. Further, the devil was persuasive enough to convince a third of the angels to follow him. Thus, he and the rebellious angels were judged and cast out of heaven. *"And the great dragon was cast out, that old serpent, called the Devil, and Satan, which deceiveth the whole world: he was cast out into the earth, and his angels were cast out with him."* (Revelation 12:9)

> SATAN AND HIS DEMONS ROAM THE EARTH, SEEKING PEOPLE TO INFLUENCE.

So, where is the devil today? He is not in hell as some suppose; he and many of his fellow fallen angels, known as demons, roam the earth. His primary goal is to oppose God and mankind. He is desperate to keep people from receiving Christ as their Savior, and he loves to afflict God's people who are faithful to their Creator. The devil is a spiritual foe like no other.

We naturally assume that Satan has an advantage over us, just as a cat has an advantage over a mouse. Surprisingly enough, this is not always true. Paul warned the Corinthians, *"Lest Satan should get an advantage of us: for we are not ignorant of his devices."* (II Corinthians 2:11) He seeks to *"get an advantage"* because he does not currently have it. You may say, "But Satan is more powerful than we are." He may be more powerful than you, but he is not more powerful than the Holy Spirit Who lives within every saved person. The apostle John said, *"Ye are of God, little children, and have overcome them: because greater is he that is in you, than he that is in the world."* (I John 4:4) I read about two teens who got into a fight on a basketball court. One boy left the court and returned with a gun to shoot the other guy. He had lost the fight and wanted an advantage, so he got a gun. The devil is just as extreme and dirty in his tactics. Because we already have the advantage, he seeks to take that advantage away by bringing out his weapons of temptation. If he can draw us away by fleshly temptations, the influence of the Holy Spirit in our lives is quenched and thereby dissolves any advantage we have. (See I Thessalonians 5:19.) Thus, we become vulnerable to Satan's onslaught! Just remember that a step into sin is a leap from God's protection.

The devil also realizes that we are more than conquerors while we have the Sword of the Lord in our hands. The Word of God is likened to a sword, which can fend off the attacks of Satan. (See Ephesians 6:17 and Hebrews 4:12.) So, if Satan can keep you from reading the Bible or hearing preaching, he succeeds in disarming you. It is no light thing to enter a battle without a weapon, and the Christian soldier must be equipped with God's Sword in his hand daily. The devil cleverly keeps you up late at night or clutters your morning schedule so you have little time to spend in the Bible. Therefore, you must guard that time to maintain your advantage.

Because sin is addictive, Satan uses it to control people. *"Know ye not, that to whom ye yield yourselves servants to obey, his servants ye are to whom ye obey...?"* (Romans 6:16) Once he has you in bondage, he has no intentions of letting you go. Isaiah 14:17 says that Lucifer *"opened not the house of his prisoners."* Knowing that he is a hard taskmaster, isn't it better to serve Jesus instead?

How can we defeat such a powerful opponent? *"Submit yourselves therefore to God. Resist the devil, and he will flee from you."* (James 4:7) Satan is stronger than you are, but God is stronger than he is. Therefore, the key to victory is to stay close to the Lord for protection. Allow me to illustrate. On my way home from school one day as a child, I got into a fight with a bigger boy and found myself on the ground getting punched out. All of a sudden, the boy stopped hitting me, looked down the path, and suddenly got off of me. Wondering what happened, I also looked down the path and was overjoyed at what I saw! My big brother was also on his way home from school, and he was bigger than the boy I was fighting. I learned that my brother's presence brought safety. The same is true in our fight with the devil. He would like to beat you senseless, but He backs down when we are close to the Lord. Because we do not have sufficient strength in ourselves, we are told to *"be strong in the Lord, and in the power of his might."* (Ephesians 6:10) Consider a few practical things you can do to guard against Satan's attacks.

*Shut the door.* *"Neither give place to the devil."* (Ephesians 4:27) The devil wants to gain an entrance into your life, but you must keep the door shut! Pursuing activities that you know are sinful leaves an opening for Satan to influence you. Once he gets his foot in the door, it is difficult to close. Steer clear of every evil matter.

*Be alert.* Don't be caught off guard by the enemy. Living a careless life as a soldier can be deadly. Consider I Peter 5:8 once again: *"Be sober, be vigilant; because your adversary the devil, as a roaring lion, walketh about, seeking whom he may devour."* We are told to be sober and vigilant. To be sober is to be cautious and serious-minded. To be vigilant is to be awake and watchful. A guard asleep at his post is susceptible to a lurking enemy, and a Christian who is dozing is an easy target for Satan.

*Get equipped.* While wearing the armor of God, you have invincible protection. Ephesians 6:13 exhorts, *"Wherefore take unto you the whole armour of God, that ye may be able to withstand in the evil day, and having done all, to stand."* The pieces of the armor are listed in the next five verses and correspond to things we should do in our daily lives: tell the truth, be righteous, spread the gospel, have faith, be assured of our salvation, read the Word of God, and pray. (Ephesians 6:14-18)

> GOD'S ARMOR WILL PROTECT YOU.

Failure to put on one piece of armor makes you vulnerable to attack. Telling a lie or missing your Bible reading time leaves you unprotected. Therefore, we must strive to live a consistent life of holiness for the Lord each day.

*Push back.* Both Peter and James exhort us to *"resist"* the devil. (See I Peter 5:9 and James 4:7.) To resist someone means you go against them. Instead of being in agreement with the devil, you must learn to say, "No." Nobody will deny that Satan's temptations are quite attractive, but we must resist. Say, "No," every time! That means you will feel deprived of friendships, fun, and entertainment that the enemy offers.

To summarize, let us remember that the devil is a powerful enemy who seeks to destroy us. However, we do not have to fear as long as we stay close to the Lord and follow His instructions for the battle. Living a holy life, clinging to the Sword (the Word of God), and praying to our Captain will keep us safe indeed. Be alert and watch for the assault of the devil, and you shall be able to fend him off in the power of the Lord.

## BEWARE OF THE FLESH

It is bad enough to have Satan against us, but we have another enemy that never leaves us—our flesh. Enemies are more dangerous when you are unaware of who they are. Therefore, it is vital that we realize our flesh can be a formidable foe.

What is the flesh? Certainly, it is the body that houses your soul, but it is more than that. The flesh carries with it a sinful, corrupt nature called the old man. Paul describes it in Ephesians 4:22, *"That ye put off concerning the former conversation the old man, which is corrupt according to the deceitful lusts."* Those deceitful lusts work in our body causing us to desire sin.

*The flesh is corrupt.* Paul struggled with his flesh and said, *"For I know that in me (that is, in my flesh,) dwelleth no good thing."* (Romans 7:18) It is humbling to admit that there is nothing good within us. There is no "spark of divinity" within as some teach. We are inherently bad people, not good. Your flesh likes to sin! Your eyes like to look at things they should not see, your tongue utters things it should not say, and your ears long to listen to things that are forbidden by God. Lying, gossip, and lust are all desires of the flesh. Nobody has to teach small children to touch something that is forbidden. They have a built-in desire for evil in their flesh, and that passion grows as they get older.

*The flesh is opposed to God.* The word *carnal* is another word used to describe fleshly. Romans 8:7 says, *"...the carnal mind is enmity against God: for it is not subject to the law of God, neither indeed can be."* Your flesh is in direct opposition to God! It does not want to obey His Word, and that is why you find it difficult to do what is right sometimes. Your spiritual enemy, the flesh, hinders you from pleasing God. However, this gives us no excuse to sin. We must realize that the flesh is a dangerous enemy.

*Everyone's flesh is weak.* As Jesus spoke to His closest disciples, He warned them of the feebleness of the flesh, *"Watch and pray, that ye enter not into temptation: the spirit indeed is willing, but <u>the flesh is weak</u>."* (Matthew 26:41) All flesh is weak—mine and yours. Even the most notable heroes in the Bible had weak flesh. The great apostle Paul considered himself to be *"less than the least of all saints."* (Ephesians 3:8) Who are we to think that we are any stronger? The weaknesses of the flesh abound: laziness, fear, anger, lust, envy, drunkenness, fornication, *etc.* One person's flesh may be weaker in one area than another person's, but all flesh is weak!

*The flesh is dishonest and evil.* The Lord said, *"The heart is deceitful above all things, and desperately wicked: who can know it?"* (Jeremiah 17:9) Your *"heart"* lies and cannot be trusted. People often say, "Follow your heart." Don't ever listen to that advice! The heart leads us astray. It tells us that sin is okay and continually justifies selfish ambitions.

I hope you are beginning to see the depravity of the flesh. Although God created the first man with a sinless body, after the choice for sin was made, corruption entered the human race. Unfortunately, that wayward character has been inherited by all of us. Therefore, we must acknowledge that our flesh, as much as we may like it, is a powerful enemy of the soul.

The flesh can only be overcome by the Holy Spirit of God, Who resides in the heart of every believer. You must understand that a great war rages within every child of God—the flesh vs. the Spirit. *"For the flesh lusteth against the Spirit, and the Spirit against the flesh: and these are contrary the one to the other: so that ye cannot do the things that ye would."* (Galatians 5:17) When the flesh dominates, it leads to many sins. (See Galatians 5:19-21.) However, when the Spirit is allowed to reign, He produces wonderful attributes that replace the sinful works of the flesh. Paul enumerates the fruit of the Spirit in Galatians 5:22-23, *"...love, joy, peace, longsuffering, gentleness, goodness, faith, meekness, temperance..."* What characterizes your life: the works of the flesh or the Spirit?

> A GREAT BATTLE RAGES WITHIN.

You determine who wins the battle in your heart. If you yield to the flesh, it takes over; but if you yield to the Spirit, He will control you. We are told, *"Walk in the Spirit, and ye shall not fulfil the lust of the flesh."* (Galatians 5:16) If you begin to feed the flesh with ungodly sights, sounds, and influences, don't be surprised when you live a defeated Christian life. However, if you begin to feast on the Word of God, you will find it much easier to have victory over the flesh. Paul said that *"the inward man is renewed day by day."* (II Corinthians 4:16) That is why it is vital to read your Bible daily. Finally, to be victorious over the flesh, you must learn to tell it, "No." Just as Jesus was crucified on the cross, we must put to death the sinful desires that arise in our hearts. *"And they that are Christ's have crucified the flesh with the affections and lusts."* (Galatians 5:24)

## BEWARE OF THE WORLD

Our third enemy, the world, works hand in hand with the first two enemies we have already discussed. Satan uses the things in the world to appeal to our flesh. Unfortunately, this strong alliance has defeated many Christians who were unprepared for the battle.

The word *world* is used in a couple of different ways in the Bible. First, it describes the people who reside on earth. Jesus loves all of the people in the world and died to demonstrate that love. *"For God so loved the world, that he gave his only begotten Son, that whosoever believeth in him should not perish, but have everlasting life."* (John 3:16) Surely, if Jesus loves the world, we ought to also.

However, the second use of the term *world* refers to the human system that is opposed to God. In this case, we are not to love it but hate it. *"Love not the world, neither the things that are in the world. If any man love the world, the love of the Father is not in him."* (I John 2:15) So, we are to love the people of the world but are commanded to hate the world system that belittles our precious Lord, the Bible, and holiness.

All of the things that are of the world's system are evil. The apostle John explains, *"For all that is in the world, the lust of the flesh, and the lust of the eyes, and the pride of life, is not of the Father, but is of the world."* (I John 2:16) The world produces lustful things that appeal to your flesh. Therefore, it is your enemy. A good Christian must guard his life from the world's influence. Unfortunately, most believers are swayed by the world more than they realize. The world pumps its filth into the mind through television, movies, music, books, radio, cell phones, and the internet. Unguarded use of any of these avenues is an open invitation for the enemy to enter your heart and home. Beware!

As stated earlier, Satan is the one who energizes the world's assault on God and His people. The Bible clearly names the devil as *"the god of this world"* who has *"blinded the minds of them which believe not."* (II Corinthians 4:4) Although he is not the absolute ruler over creation, he is certainly the organizer of the evil we witness around the world. Satan promotes sex, murder, blasphemy, and obscene language through music, television, and the movies. He influences filmmakers, musicians, and fashion designers to create an appetite for filth and immorality. He has attacked life through abortion, euthanasia, and suicide. Further, his efforts to destroy the family unit have included divorce, adultery, redefining marriage, and abandonment of child discipline. In short, Satan orchestrates the affairs of this world's system to attack all that is decent and godly.

> SATAN APPEALS TO YOUR FLESH THROUGH THINGS IN THE WORLD.

Satan will try to appeal to you in three main ways in order to engage your flesh and spoil your relationship with God. They are listed in I John 2:16, *"...the lust of the flesh, and the lust of the eyes, and the pride of life."* First, he appeals through *"the lust of the flesh."* The devil likes to offer things that make people feel "good." The effects of drugs and alcohol provide temporary feelings of pleasure and relief, but they also produce horrible consequences. Rather than yielding to the lusts of the flesh, why not yield to God and receive lasting peace and joy?

Second, Satan charms us with *"the lust of the eyes."* In the Garden of Eden, Adam and Eve found out that some things appear good but are actually deadly. Eating the forbidden fruit led to spiritual death and separation from God. Even though smoking looks "cool," it has killed countless thousands. Covetousness begins by gazing enviously at things we hope to attain. Once the lust of the eyes is engaged and covetousness takes over, people go headlong into debt. Satan tries to create havoc in every area of your life. Beware of *"the lust of the eyes,"* and control what you gaze upon.

Third, *"the pride of life"* is a tool quite often utilized by the devil. Pride causes us to seek our own way instead of God's. What makes us rebel against authority? Pride. The attitude of arrogance will lead to a refusal to accept correction. Pride is so hideous that it is the reason Lucifer was cast out of heaven, and the world has never been the same since pride entered into it. The devil wants to destroy you, and he knows the best way to do it is to appeal to your pride. That is why God warned us about it—*"Pride goeth before destruction."* (Proverbs 16:18)

You must realize that the world is your enemy, and it is run by Satan. You literally enter a battlefield every day. Therefore, you must be prepared for the attacks that this world will wage against you and your family. Be aware that your weak flesh will be tempted by experiences, sights, and haughtiness. There is no need to fear, however, because we are promised victory over the world. *"For whatsoever is born of God overcometh the world: and this is the victory that overcometh the world, even our faith."* (I John 5:4)

# Chapter Six

# Go to Church!

*"Not forsaking the assembling of ourselves together, as the manner of some is; but exhorting one another: and so much the more, as ye see the day approaching."* Hebrews 10:25

Not many years ago, it was common for people to attend church on Sunday. In fact, the majority of stores and restaurants would not even open on the Lord's Day so that folks could go to church. Today, things have changed! Now, Sundays are seen as a time for relaxation, shopping, sporting events, projects around the house, and getaways. It is surprising to meet so many people who have never even gone to church or who only go a couple of times a year. Because many people do not know much about the local church, it is helpful to answer a few questions about it.

## What is a Church?

To many, a church is merely a building decorated with a cross and/or a steeple. However, a church is not a building. The word *church* in the New Testament means *to call out from*. It refers to a group of people who have been called out of the world and are united in a particular assembly. The churches in the Bible were local groups of believers. No big universal church exists on earth.

Further, not all people who attend a church are an actual part of it. Only those who have received Jesus as their Savior and been baptized are eligible to become members of a church. In every church, there are members and attenders. God's plan is that each person joins a Biblical church after being saved. In the first church at Jerusalem, new believers had a great desire to be a part of the church. *"Then they that gladly received his word were baptized: and the same day there were added unto them about three thousand souls."* (Acts 2:41) We can clearly see that God wants people to be *"added"* to His churches. After joining the church, you become part of the church family. So, now that we have discovered that a church is a group of united believers and not just a building, let's move on to the next question.

## WHY SHOULD WE GO TO CHURCH?

The reasons for going to church are too numerous to list in just a couple of pages. However, we will consider a few of them.

*First, we are commanded to go to church.* If for no other reason, we should go simply because God said to do it. *"Not forsaking the assembling of ourselves together..."* (Hebrews 10:25) People argue that they can have church at home, but God says we must be *"assembling...together."* That means listening to preachers on the radio, television, or computer is no substitute for church attendance. Something special happens in a service when God's people get together. Jesus said, *"...where two or three are gathered together in my name, there am I in the midst of them."* (Matthew 18:20) At church, the Lord meets with His people and speaks through His Spirit to their hearts, but you miss all of that when you stay home.

*Second, church is a place to gain spiritual nourishment.* God gives pastors to churches to feed people spiritually. He promised, *"And I will give you pastors according to mine heart, which shall feed you with knowledge and understanding."* (Jeremiah 3:15) Members of a church are God's sheep, and He cares for them by leading pastors to know what the sheep need to hear from the Bible. When you fail to be in church, you miss the meal that God had prepared for you. The truth is, many of God's people suffer from spiritual malnutrition.

> GOD GIVES PASTORS TO FEED THE PEOPLE IN THE CHURCH.

When you don't eat enough food, you get weak; and when you fail to get fed at church, you will not have the strength to fight off temptation or discouragement.

*Third, church provides the right kind of fellowship.* The people with whom you surround yourself will affect your life—for good or for bad. By going to church, you gain new friends who can be a tremendous help to your life. In fact, fellow believers have already faced problems, trials, and temptations similar to the ones that you currently face. God, in His wisdom, has designed the church so that members can encourage one another. He comforts us *"...that we may be able to comfort them which are in any trouble, by the comfort wherewith we ourselves are comforted of God."* (II Corinthians 1:4) Where can you find godly friends to help you in your Christian life? At church!

*Fourth, you have a job to do.* Every member of a church has been given gifts to use within the church. (See Romans 12:6-8.) Accordingly, if you are not there to do your job, the rest of the members suffer. *"So we, being many, are one body in Christ, and every one members one of another."* (Romans 12:5) The church is likened to a body, and every part supplies what is needed to keep the body running smoothly. (See Ephesians 4:16.) What happens when one part of your body gets injured? Your whole life is affected. If you break your leg, your arms have to do more work with the crutches, your other leg carries a heavier load, and many of your muscles begin to ache. In like manner, the church is slowed down when other members have to take up the slack of missing members. Even if you feel inadequate, jump in and learn to do your part!

*Fifth, church provides spiritual protection.* Many false prophets preach on television, host radio programs, and write books. Such men are called *"wolves in sheep's clothing,"* and they lead multitudes away with false doctrine. Thankfully, God gives you a pastor to warn you about and protect you from such hurtful teachings. In fact, the word *pastor* means *shepherd*, and one of the jobs of a shepherd is to guard the sheep. Therefore, you need to be in church so your pastor can teach, guide, and counsel you. Too many people have their own opinions about spiritual matters because they never became faithful to God's established institution—the local church.

I hope you are convinced of your need to be in church. Now, let's see the right way to go to a church service.

## How Should We Attend Church?

The devil would love to stop you from attending church; but if he cannot do that, he will attempt to get you there with the wrong attitude. It is amazing how many fights between husbands and wives arise on the way to church! A couple can get along all week, but Satan hurls a few of his fiery darts at them just at the "right" time. Perhaps you have never given much thought to how you should attend a church service. Let's consider a few ideas that can help you get the most out of going to church.

*First, be positive.* David said, *"I was glad when they said unto me, Let us go into the house of the LORD."* (Psalm 122:1) Going to church should be a joyful experience. If you have to drag yourself to church with a "Do I have to go?" attitude, you are not going to get much out of it. Look forward to what God has in store for you. He may have a promise for you to claim to help you in your trial, a warning to prevent you from a serious mistake, or a person for you to assist in some way. To a good Christian, going to church is a breath of fresh air to get away from the wickedness of the world and enjoy the presence of God. I pity those who have the "last one in and first one out" philosophy. Learn to look forward to church attendance.

> GOING TO CHURCH SHOULD BE A JOYFUL EXPERIENCE.

*Second, be prepared.* Sunday is the most important day of the week—treat it that way. In fact, it is called *"the Lord's day."* (Revelation 1:10) It is sad to hear people excuse missing church with statements like, "Oh, I didn't have anything to wear for church." If you had an important meeting with a senator, you would take time to choose the right outfit. Let's not forget that we are meeting Someone far more important when we go to church. Be prepared to meet with the Lord.

*Third, be prompt.* Did you know that God is never late? He created time and keeps all of His appointments, and He expects us to be on time for church. The Lord said, *"Let all things be done decently and in order."* (I Corinthians 14:40) If you are ten minutes late for church every week, it adds up to five hundred and twenty minutes in a year's time. That is a lot of time to be without God's instruction!

*Fourth, be prayerful.* The most important thing you can do before entering a church service is to pray and ask God to speak to your heart. The Psalmist said, *"Open thou mine eyes, that I may behold wondrous things out of thy law."* (Psalm 119:18) The reason we fail to get much from a sermon is because we fail to ask God to teach us anything. James said, *"...ye have not, because ye ask not."* (James 4:2) You can pray, *"Search me"* (Psalm 139:23), *"Lead me"* (Psalm 25:5), *"Teach me"* (Psalm 25:4, Psalm 143:10), and *"Be clear"* (Psalm 51:4). God delights to reveal wonderful truths to His children. In fact, He encourages us, *"Call unto me, and I will answer thee, and shew thee great and mighty things, which thou knowest not."* (Jeremiah 33:3) The next time you go to church, whisper a prayer and listen for the Lord's answer!

# Chapter Seven

# Tell Others

*"And he said unto them, Go ye into all the world, and preach the gospel to every creature."* Mark 16:15

Most people are familiar with the expression, "Good news travels fast." The word *gospel* means *good news*, and we ought to be quick to share with others what God has done for us. When you got saved, you found what millions of people in the world are looking for—peace, joy, and forgiveness. Why not begin to tell others what you have experienced? Our attitude should be, *"For I am not ashamed of the gospel of Christ: for it is the power of God unto salvation to every one that believeth."* (Romans 1:16) What God has done for you, He is willing to do for others, but they must first hear the good news!

## Why Should We Tell Others?

Perhaps you have never stopped to think about the reasons you should tell others about Jesus. Let's consider a few motivations for doing so.

*First, telling others demonstrates a love for the Lord.* When a young lady falls in love with the man of her dreams, all she wants to do is talk about him. It is natural to want others to know more about the people who are important to us. Do people know that you love Jesus? *"But if any man love God, the same is known of him."* (I Corinthians 8:3) It would be terrible for a man to be ashamed of his wife but even more so for a Christian to be embarrassed about Jesus. *"Be not thou therefore ashamed of the testimony of our Lord."* (II Timothy 1:8) Let your love for the Lord be known.

*Second, telling others helps those in need.* Despite the façade most people put on, the majority of people in the world are miserable inside, and the reason is that they do not have Jesus. God has already told us the condition of those without salvation, and that should motivate us to have confidence in witnessing. Consider the state of lost souls:

1. They have gone astray. *"All we like sheep have gone astray; we have turned every one to his own way; and the LORD hath laid on him the iniquity of us all."* (Isaiah 53:6)
2. They are without hope. *"That at that time ye were without Christ, being aliens from the commonwealth of Israel, and strangers from the covenants of promise, having no hope, and without God in the world..."* (Ephesians 2:12)
3. They carry guilt. *"For whosoever shall keep the whole law, and yet offend in one point, he is guilty of all."* (James 2:10)
4. They have no peace. *"There is no peace, saith the LORD, unto the wicked."* (Isaiah 48:22)

5. They are in darkness. *"To give light to them that sit in darkness and in the shadow of death, to guide our feet into the way of peace."* (Luke 1:79)
6. They are condemned. *"He that believeth on him is not condemned: but he that believeth not is condemned already, because he hath not believed in the name of the only begotten Son of God."* (John 3:18)
7. They are spiritually dead. *"And you hath he quickened, who were dead in trespasses and sins."* (Ephesians 2:1)
8. They are lost. *"For the Son of man is come to seek and to save that which was lost."* (Luke 19:10)
9. They are blind. *"In whom the god of this world hath blinded the minds of them which believe not, lest the light of the glorious gospel of Christ, who is the image of God, should shine unto them."* (II Corinthians 4:4)
10. They are destined for eternal punishment. *"And whosoever was not found written in the book of life was cast into the lake of fire."* (Revelation 20:15)

*Third, telling others is the business God told us to be involved in.* At an early age, Jesus taught the Word of God to many in the temple. When asked by His mother why He had tarried in Jerusalem, He replied, *"How is it that ye sought me? wist ye not that I must be about my Father's business?"* (Luke 2:49) His goal in life was to be about His Father's business, and His plan for His followers is to do the same. His charge to us is, *"...as my Father hath sent me, even so send I you."* (John 20:21) Let's get busy doing what the Lord has told us to do—*"Go ye into all the world, and preach the gospel to every creature."* (Mark 16:15)

*Fourth, telling others brings joy.* Do you want to be happy? As you search the Scriptures, you will repeatedly see an abundance of joy accompanying the salvation of sinners.

> GOD GIVES JOY TO THOSE WHO WITNESS FOR HIM.

Jesus spoke of the importance of abiding in Him in order to win souls, and the result of bringing people to Christ is joy. *"These things have I spoken unto you, that my joy might remain in you, and that your joy might be full."* (John 15:11) Is your joy full today? If not, start telling people about Jesus! Those who fail to witness for their Savior miss out on the joy that He wants to give.

*Fifth, telling others manifests the presence of God in your life.* Do you want to sense the Lord's closeness? Those who witness for Christ are assured of His presence. Notice His tremendous promise, *"Go ye therefore, and teach all nations...and, lo, I am with you always."* (Matthew 28:19-20) You never have to fear when you go to represent the Lord because He will be with you! When feelings of anxiety about telling others arise within your heart, you can rest upon the words, *"I am with you always."*

*Sixth, telling others earns eternal rewards.* Who wouldn't want to be rewarded in heaven? Christ spoke of lost sinners as *"fields...white already to harvest,"* and He encouraged His disciples to gather the waiting harvest. Further, He promised eternal rewards for doing so, *"And he that reapeth receiveth wages, and gathereth fruit unto life eternal."* (John 4:36) What a blessing it will be to receive heavenly wages that will last throughout eternity!

*Seventh, telling others pleases God.* The salvation of a lost soul brings great joy in heaven. As Jesus concluded the parable of the man who found the lost sheep, He revealed how happy God becomes when a sinner is saved. *"I say unto you, that likewise joy shall be in heaven over one sinner that repenteth."* (Luke 15:7)  If you want to make God happy, start telling people about salvation through Jesus. Do you believe that blessings await those who please the Lord?

## How Can We Tell Others?

The easiest way to talk to others about the Lord is to tell them your testimony. Start by telling them what God has done for you. You can share what your life was like before salvation and how Jesus changed it. Oftentimes, you will meet people who believed much like you did previously, and it is a perfect opportunity to get right into the presentation of the gospel. For example, you can say, "I used to think that keeping the Ten Commandments would get me to heaven, but I found out that it cannot. May I share with you what I learned?"

The purpose of giving your testimony is to magnify the Lord, and when people see what He did for you, they are often encouraged that He can do the same for them. You can then begin to share Scripture that will help them find salvation. Let's consider some key passages that will assist you in presenting the gospel.

## What Should We Say to Others?

Before we get started, you must understand that there are hundreds of verses you can use to explain salvation. The ones listed below simply provide a good place to start. The most important thing is to allow the Lord to guide you as you speak to others. Although each gospel presentation may vary slightly, here are the key points you need to stress:

1. God loves you.
   - ✓ *"For God so loved the world, that he gave his only begotten Son, that whosoever believeth in him should not perish, but have everlasting life."* (John 3:16)
2. Although God loves you, He hates your sin.
   - ✓ *"For all have sinned, and come short of the glory of God..."* (Romans 3:23)
   - ✓ *"...God is angry with the wicked every day."* (Psalm 7:11)
3. God has promised to punish sin.
   - ✓ *"For the wages of sin is death; but the gift of God is eternal life through Jesus Christ our Lord."* (Romans 6:23)
   - ✓ *"And death and hell were cast into the lake of fire. This is the second death."* (Revelation 20:14)
4. Surprisingly, some things you think will save you will not.
   a. The Ten Commandments cannot save you.
      - ✓ *"Therefore we conclude that a man is justified by faith without the deeds of the law."* (Romans 3:28)
      - ✓ *"But that no man is justified by the law in the sight of God, it is evident: for, The just shall live by faith."* (Galatians 3:11)
   b. Baptism cannot save you.
      - ✓ *"...not the putting away of the filth of the flesh, but the answer of a good conscience toward God"* (I Peter 3:21)
      - ✓ *"...the blood of Jesus Christ his Son cleanseth us from all sin."* (I John 1:7)

  c. Good works cannot save you.
- ✓ *"For by grace are ye saved through faith; and that not of yourselves: it is the gift of God: Not of works, lest any man should boast."* (Ephesians 2:8-9)
- ✓ *"Not by works of righteousness which we have done, but according to his mercy he saved us, by the washing of regeneration, and renewing of the Holy Ghost"* (Titus 3:5)

5. You must trust Jesus to save you. (A person must be willing to repent of his sin and self-righteousness in order to receive Christ as Savior.)
   - ✓ *"But as many as received him, to them gave he power to become the sons of God, even to them that believe on his name"* (John 1:12)
   - ✓ *"Jesus saith unto him, I am the way, the truth, and the life: no man cometh unto the Father, but by me."* (John 14:6)
6. Would you like to receive Jesus as your Savior right now?
   - ✓ *"For whosoever shall call upon the name of the Lord shall be saved."* (Romans 10:13)

  Whew! That may seem like a lot to learn, but you will be surprised how quickly you will pick it up. You may want to write these verses on a 3 x 5 card and place it in your Bible so you have easy access to them when you are witnessing. Don't worry if people see you looking at your list of verses. Just tell them, "This is so important that I don't want to skip anything!" Some people make notes in their Bible to indicate which verse to turn to next. The most important thing you can do is to trust the Lord to guide what you say.

## When Should We Tell Others?

We should work while there is time. Some people may only get one opportunity to hear the gospel. Jesus had the right attitude about reaching the unsaved, *"I must work the works of him that sent me, while it is day: the night cometh, when no man can work."* (John 9:4) Your days are limited to tell the good news, and the days of the unsaved are numbered to hear it. It's time to get busy!

The apostle Paul told us, *"Preach the word; be instant in season, out of season."* (II Timothy 4:2) Good churches have times scheduled for soulwinning, and I like to consider such times as being *"in season."* Any opportunities that arise outside of scheduled soulwinning times can be considered *"out of season."* In other words, we should be ready to witness for Christ at any time, whether it is in our schedule or not. We must *"be ready always to give an answer to every man that asketh you a reason of the hope that is in you."* (I Peter 3:15)

## Where Should We Tell Others?

A great advantage about witnessing is that we can talk to people anywhere. Paul's testimony was, *"I...have shewed you, and have taught you publickly, and from house to house."* (Acts 20:20) He taught in the market, schools, prison, and houses. While conducting your daily activities, you can pass out tracts and look for opportunities to direct people to Christ. Whether you are shopping, at the doctor's office, or getting fuel, someone may be willing to hear about the Lord. As Paul went *"from house to house,"* so can we through our church's organized soulwinning program. This allows us to come into contact with people we would not normally meet. So, whether it be cashier, neighbor, relative, or stranger, we have almost unlimited prospects to talk to.

## WHO SHOULD TELL OTHERS?

While it is true that some people are more outgoing than others, we all have an obligation to witness. Psalm 107:2 says, *"Let the redeemed of the LORD say so."* If you are saved, God expects you to witness.

God has equipped you with a unique personality that He wants to use. Never think you are ill-equipped to speak about Jesus. You know more than any other person what the Lord has done for you, and your testimony can be a powerful influence on the lives of others. Further, you have exclusive opportunities to share the gospel with people in your sphere of influence—whether at work, in the neighborhood, among family members, or in daily errands. You know people that others in the church do not know, and it is your responsibility to share the good news with them. This should motivate you to pray for and notice opportunities to tell people about the news that will set them free.

If you think you don't have enough Bible knowledge, think again. It is not a matter of sharing what you don't know, but what you do know. If you are saved, you know something! As time goes on, you will learn more Bible verses to use in presenting the gospel; but for now, just share what you know. Even new converts have the promise of *"the Lord working with them."* (Mark 16:20) Having the Lord with you is better than all the knowledge in the world!

What if nobody had told you about Jesus? You wouldn't have forgiveness, peace, joy, or a home in heaven. Aren't you glad someone told you? Someone like you is waiting to hear the good news. Ask God to lead you to that one today.

# Appendix

# Terms to Know

When you first start attending church, you may hear some unfamiliar terminology. We want you to understand what is going on in your church. So, here are a few common terms explained:

**altar** – In the Bible, the altar was a place of sacrifice. However, it has symbolic meaning, too. When a person makes a public decision for the Lord by kneeling in prayer at the front of the auditorium, it is considered as done at the "altar."
**bus meeting** – Churches who send buses into the community usually have a weekly meeting to plan and pray for the outreach.
**business meeting** – Many details of church business are presented to the members at such meetings.
**canvassing** – Going from door to door looking for new prospects is considered a canvass.
**communion** – The communion service is also called the Lord's Supper. It is an ordinance conducted by the local church to remember the sacrificial death of Christ.
**deacon** – The word *deacon* means servant. Thus, deacons serve the church by ministering to the members. They work under the direction of the pastor.
**devotions** – A daily time of Bible reading and prayer is referred to as devotions because it is an opportunity to devote ourselves to the Lord.
**discipleship** – A disciple is a follower of Jesus. The process of becoming a disciple is typically called discipleship.
**family devotions** – Just as individuals should spend time with the Lord, so should families. The man, being the head of the house, should lead his family in a short time of Bible study and prayer.

**fellowship** – Activities involving fellow believers for the purpose of encouragement are often called times of fellowship.

**follow-up** – A church will often follow up on visitors who have attended in order to help them with their relationship with God.

**invitation** – The time at the conclusion of a sermon is often called an invitation because people are invited to either come to Christ for salvation or make a new commitment to God.

**Junior Church** – This is a church service designed for children to learn on their age level.

**ministries** – The church has many ways that it serves its members and people in the community. Such opportunities to serve God are known as church ministries.

**ordinances** – The local church has only two ceremonies that it performs: baptism and the Lord's Supper. Both ordinances depict the sacrifice that Christ made on the cross. Neither have any saving power but are only symbolic.

**pastor** – The leader of the church is known as the pastor. The word *pastor* means shepherd. His job is to lead, feed, warn, and protect the sheep, which are the members of the church. Other terms for the same position in the Bible are bishop, elder, and overseer.

**prayer meeting** – Most churches provide times for the members to pray to God together.

**revival** – The word *revive* means to make alive. When God breathes a new sense of life and spiritual well-being into an individual or a church, it is considered revival.

**separation** – God expects His children to separate from evil influences and associations.

**soulwinning** – This term refers to bringing a soul to Christ. We are to tell people about Jesus and win them over to Him from the devil.

**standards** – God's Word provides principles to live by, and standards are guidelines that we form to help us obey God.

**Sunday School** – This important teaching service typically starts before the main church service on Sunday mornings. It is designed to provide instruction from the Bible to assist in daily living. Sunday School is for all ages and is divided accordingly.

**visitation** – This is a time for people to visit others who need encouragement and Bible instruction.

**worship** – Typically, worship carries the idea of glorifying God. We are to *"worship him in spirit and in truth."* (John 4:24) Because truth refers to the Bible, a worship service typically centers on preaching—not music.